Let's Play Tag!

 Read the Page

 Read the Story

 Repeat

 Stop

⭐ Game

⭐ Level 1   ⭐⭐ Level 2   ⭐⭐⭐ Level 3

TO USE THIS BOOK WITH THE TAG™ READER you must download audio from the LeapFrog Connect application. The LeapFrog Connect application can be installed from the CD provided with your Tag Reader or at leapfrog.com/tag.

Miss Spider's Tea Party

paintings and verse by David Kirk

SCHOLASTIC INC.   CALLAWAY ARTS & ENTERTAINMENT

One lonely spider sipped her tea,
And wished for friendly company.

Two timid beetles, Ike and May,
Shrieked, "My, oh my!" and dashed away.

Three fireflies flew inside that night,
Their spirits high, their tails alight.

They spied the web and squeaked in fear,
"We'd better get away from here!"

 Four bumblebees buzzed by outside.
"Please come to tea!" Miss Spider cried.

They growled, "We will not take our tea
With anyone so spidery."

 Five jolly faces bobbed and peered.
Miss Spider smiled. Her heart was cheered.

But then, alas! she found those mugs
Belonged to painted rubber bugs.

 Some ants strode in, they numbered six,
But ants with spiders will not mix.

She brewed them tea from leaves and roses,
The six proud ants turned up their noses.

Among the flowers, in bright disguise,
Were seven dainty butterflies.

Miss Spider, watching from the wall,
Was not aware of them at all.

The tea table was set for eight
With saucers, cups, and silver plate.

The cakes were fresh, the service gleamed,
Yet no one would arrive, it seemed.

Nine spotted moths kept safe and warm
In shelter from a thunderstorm.

They stood beneath the window sash
And watched the jagged lightning flash.

Miss Spider dropped down on a thread,
A silver tray above her head.

She'd hoped to please them, but instead . . .
They screamed and flew away in dread!

"They've left me all alone," she cried.
She heard a cough there by her side.

So cold and wet—a frightened moth.
She dried him with her checkered cloth.

Ten tiny steaming cups of tea
Were perched upon Miss Spider's knee.
They talked and snacked on tea and pie

22

Until his tiny wings were dry.
Then lifting him with tender care,
She tossed him gently in the air.

He told his friends, that afternoon,
All gathered in the dining room,
Eleven insects came to tea

To share Miss Spider's courtesy.
Twelve flowers were their gift to say,
"We've heard you're kind. Come on, let's play!"

1   2   3   4   5

Bug Count!

6   7   8   9   10

one

two

three

four

five

six

seven

eight

nine

ten

fire

flower

bow

bird

pot

cake

firefly   teacup

birdhouse   cupcake

fly

tea

cup

house

butter

rain

rainbow   teapot

flowerpot   butterfly

Playtime!

trampoline   seesaw   portrait

paintbrush   guitar   xylophone

hopscotch   paddle   palette

canoe

w

s

b

h

r

sing   wing   ring

bat   hat   sat

ay

ing

at

ug

bug   hug   rug
way   ray   say